MS ROSAMOND D BRENNER
310 LINDEN AVE
WILMETTE IL 60091

YO-CUN-393

DAYS OF RIḌVÁN
A Compilation

Other Books in this Series:

The Passing of 'Abdu'l-Bahá: *A Compilation*
The Ascension of Bahá'u'lláh: *A Compilation*
Declaration of the Báb: *A Compilation*
Martyrdom of the Báb: *A Compilation*

Forthcoming

Day of the Covenant: *A Compilation*
Naw-Rúz: New Day: *A Compilation*

THE MOSQUE OF IMÁM MÚSÁ
in Baghdad. circa 1860.

The Bettmann Archive

DAYS OF RIḌVÁN

A Compilation

※

KALIMÁT PRESS
Los Angeles

Copyright © 1992 by Kalimát Press.
All Rights Reserved.
Manufactured in the United States of America.

Library of Congress Cataloging-in-Publication Data

The Days of Riḍván: a compilation.
p. cm.
Includes bibliographical references.
ISBN 0-933770-85-5 : $14.95
1. Riḍván (Bahá'í festival).   I. Bahá'u'lláh, 1817-1892.
BP385.D39   1992
297'.9336—dc20

Cover design by Dan Cook

Acknowledgements

The following works are reprinted by permission: From the National Spiritual Assembly of the Bahá'ís of the United States—By Bahá'u'lláh, *Gleanings from the Writings of Bahá'u'lláh*, Copyright 1952, ©1976. By 'Abdu'l-Bahá, *The Promulgation of Universal Peace*, Copyright ©1982. By Shoghi Effendi, *The World Order of Bahá'u'lláh*, Copyright 1938, ©1955, 1974; *God Passes By*, Copyright 1944, ©1971, 1974.

Contents

Preface ix

Tablets Revealed for Riḍván
by Bahá'u'lláh 1

Days of Riḍván
words of 'Abdu'l-Bahá 21

The Declaration of Bahá'u'lláh's Mission
by Shoghi Effendi 31

Accounts of the Garden of Riḍván
  The Account of
    the Greatest Holy Leaf 49
  The Spoken Chronicle of
    Mírzá Asadu'lláh Káshání............... 57
  The Memoirs of
    Ustád Muḥammad-'Alí Salmání 63

Appendix................................. 69

Sources 73

Preface

The Festival of Riḍván (April 21–May 2) termed by Bahá'u'lláh the *"Most Great Festival"* and the *"King of Festivals"* provides the occasion for the holiest days of the Bahá'í year. The first, the ninth, and the twelfth days of Riḍván are Bahá'í Holy Days on which work should be suspended. Coming within a few days of each other, these Holy Days mark the high point of the Bahá'í year.

The Riḍván Festival commemorates the anniversary of Bahá'u'lláh's sojourn in the garden of Najíb Pasha, outside Baghdad, during the twelve days before His banishment to Istanbul in 1863. The weeks before Bahá'u'lláh's retirement to this garden had been tragically sorrowful ones for His friends and family. Informed of the government's order which would remove Bahá'u'lláh from Baghdad and tear Him away from most of them forever, they mourned and lamented, crowding in and around His house in large numbers. Knowledge of the inevitable departure brought them nothing but sadness and despair.

However, it was on this occasion that Bahá'u'lláh chose to make a private declaration of His station to a few of the believers, who immediately accepted His claim. With this action, Bahá'u'lláh transformed the occasion of His banishment to Istanbul from tragedy into triumph. Today, the eve of Bahá'u'lláh's banishment from Baghdad is commemorated each year by Bahá'í communities around the world, not as a time of sorrow or regret, but as a festival of great joy. The holiday stands as a demonstration of the power of the Manifestation of God to create good from evil, bring forth light from darkness, and win victory from seeming defeat.

Bahá'u'lláh's declaration of His mission in the Garden of Riḍván gave new faith to the handful of believers whom He chose to hear this new message. Moreover, it infused the entire gathering in the garden with joy and life. Even those who were completely unaware of the declaration felt a sense of happiness and joy. These feelings are reclaimed by the believers each year during the celebrations of the Most Great Festival.

The Riḍván period has also been designated, by the Guardian of the Bahá'í Faith, as the time when Bahá'ís around the world must elect the institutions that will serve them through the coming year. Elections for local Spiritual Assemblies (in every locality where Bahá'ís reside), and National Spiritual Assemblies (in every country) are held each year during the twelve days of Riḍván, preferably (in the case of

PREFACE

the local institutions) on the first day of Riḍván, as it is the holiest day of the Bahá'í year. Every five years, the Universal House of Justice is elected during this same period. In gathering to say prayers and silently cast their ballots for the institutions that will guide them through the year, Bahá'ís symbolically renew their covenant with Bahá'u'lláh and redeem His declaration in the Garden of Riḍván, affirming the structure of a living, world community established in His name.

This book draws together a selection of passages from the Bahá'í Sacred Writings which can be used at Holy Day celebrations and other occasions during the Riḍván period. The first section presents Tablets of Bahá'u'lláh revealed specifically for Riḍván. These include the majestic discourse in which the Manifestation symbolically addresses His pen as the instrument of the Revelation of His words, and proclaims His station: *"The Divine Springtime is come, O Most Exalted Pen . . ."*

Next are provided passages from the talks and Tablets of 'Abdu'l-Bahá which are associated with Riḍván. These include: a brief explanation of Bahá'u'lláh's declaration in the Garden of Riḍván, a talk delivered by 'Abdu'l-Bahá on the first day of Riḍván while he was in America (April 21, 1912), and a

PREFACE

Tablet addressed to an individual believer who asked specifically for words to be read at the Riḍván celebration.

Following this is the story of Bahá'u'lláh's banishment from Baghdad and his consequent Declaration as told by Shoghi Effendi in *God Passes By*. The Guardian writes:

> *Of the exact circumstances attending that epoch-making Declaration we, alas, are but scantily informed. The words Bahá'u'lláh actually uttered on that occasion, the manner of His Declaration, the reaction it produced, its impact on Mírzá Yaḥyá, the identity of those who were privileged to hear Him, are shrouded in an obscurity which future historians will find it difficult to penetrate. The fragmentary description left to posterity by His chronicler Nabíl is one of the very few authentic records we possess of the memorable days He spent in that garden.*

Following this passage, he provides long quotations from Nabíl's Narrative.

Finally, the last section of the book offers three eyewitness accounts to the events in the Garden of Riḍván from Bahá'ís who were present at the time, though none of them—it seems—were privy to the private declaration of Bahá'u'lláh's messianic secret. First, from Bahá'u'lláh's daughter, Bahíyyih Khánum, is the moving account of the harried preparations in

PREFACE

the household for the journey to Istanbul. On the ninth day, she, along with other members of the Holy Family, joined Bahá'u'lláh in the Garden of Riḍván, departing with Him on the twelfth day. Second, we have the testimony of Mírzá Asadu'lláh Kashání, who tells us clearly that he did not know of Bahá'u'lláh's secret declaration. His experiences in the Garden of Riḍván were nonetheless enchanting and joyous. Finally, the memoir of Muḥammad-'Alí Salmání, Bahá'u'lláh's barber and bath attendant, one of His companions throughout His exiles. Salmání was a simple and unlettered man, naively prepared to defend Bahá'u'lláh with arms, if necessary. Even though he, too, remained unaware of his Master's full station.

It is our hope that this compilation will provide a fuller understanding of the Festival of Riḍván for the Bahá'í community and will be a ready reference to assist with the development of programs for fitting celebrations of these precious Holy Days.

—THE EDITORS

Tablets
Revealed for Riḍván
by Bahá'u'lláh

Shoghi Effendi, in God Passes By, *has collected some of Baha'u'lláh's statements concerning the significance of His Declaration in the Garden of Riḍván:*

As to the significance of that Declaration let Bahá'u'lláh Himself reveal to us its import. Acclaiming that historic occasion as the *"Most Great Festival,"* the *"King of Festivals,"* the *"Festival of God,"* He has, in His Kitáb-i-Aqdas, characterized it as the Day whereon *"all created things were immersed in the sea of purification,"* whilst in one of His specific Tablets, He has referred to it as the Day whereon *"the breezes of forgiveness were wafted over the entire creation."*

The Divine Springtime is come, O Most Exalted Pen, for the Festival of the All-Merciful is fast approaching. Bestir thyself, and magnify, before the entire creation, the name of God, and celebrate His praise, in such wise that all created things may be regenerated and made new. Speak, and hold not thy peace. The day star of blissfulness shineth above the horizon of Our name, the Blissful, inasmuch as the kingdom of the name of God hath been adorned with the ornament of the name of thy Lord, the Creator of the heavens. Arise before the nations of the earth, and arm thyself with the power of this Most Great Name, and be not of those who tarry.

Methinks that thou hast halted and movest not upon my Tablet. Could the brightness of the Divine Countenance have bewildered thee, or the idle talk of the froward filled thee with grief and paralyzed thy movement? Take heed lest anything deter thee from extolling the greatness of this Day—the Day whereon the Finger of majesty and power hath opened the seal of the Wine of Reunion, and called all who are in the heavens and all who are on the earth. Preferrest thou to tarry when the breeze announcing the Day of God hath already breathed over thee, or art thou of them that are shut out as by a veil from Him?

No veil whatever have I allowed, O Lord of all names and Creator of the heavens, to shut me from the recognition of the glories of Thy Day—the Day which is the lamp of guidance unto the whole world, and the sign of the Ancient of Days unto all them that dwell therein. My silence is by reason of the veils that have blinded Thy creatures' eyes to Thee, and my muteness is because of the impediments that have hindered Thy people from recognizing Thy truth. Thou knowest what is in me, but I know not what is in Thee. Thou art the All-Knowing, the All-Informed. By Thy name that excelleth all other names! If Thy overruling and all-compelling behest should ever reach me, it would empower me to revive the souls of all men, through Thy most exalted Word, which I have heard uttered by Thy Tongue of power in Thy Kingdom of glory. It would enable me to announce the revelation of Thy effulgent countenance wherethrough that which lay hidden from the eyes of men hath been manifested in Thy name, the Perspicuous, the sovereign Protector, the Self-Subsisting.

Canst thou discover any one but Me, O Pen, in this Day? What hath become of the creation and the manifestations thereof? What of the names and their kingdom? Whither are gone all created things, whether seen or unseen? What of the hidden secrets of the universe and its revelations? Lo, the entire creation hath passed away! Nothing remaineth except My Face, the Ever-Abiding, the Resplendent, the All-Glorious.

This is the Day whereon naught can be seen except the splendors of the Light that shineth from the face of Thy Lord, the Gracious, the Most Bountiful. Verily, We have caused every soul to expire by virtue of Our irresistible and all-subduing sovereignty. We have, then, called into being a new creation, as a token of Our grace unto men. I am, verily, the All-Bountiful, the Ancient of Days.

This is the Day whereon the unseen world crieth out: "Great is thy blessedness, O earth, for thou hast been made the foot-stool of thy God, and been chosen as the seat of His mighty throne." The realm of glory exclaimeth: "Would that my life could be sacrificed for thee, for He Who is the Beloved of the All-Merciful hath established His sovereignty upon thee, through the power of His Name that hath been promised unto all things, whether of the past or of the future." This is the Day whereon every sweet smelling thing hath derived its fragrance from the smell of My garment—a garment that hath shed its perfume upon the whole of creation. This is the Day whereon the rushing waters of everlasting life have gushed out of the Will of the All-Merciful. Haste ye, with your hearts and souls, and quaff your fill, O Concourse of the realms above!

Say: He it is Who is the Manifestation of Him Who is the Unknowable, the Invisible of the Invisibles, could ye but perceive it. He it is Who hath laid bare before you the hidden and treasured Gem, were ye to seek it. He it is Who is the one Beloved of all things, whether of the past or of the future. Would that ye might set your hearts and hopes upon Him!

We have heard the voice of thy pleading, O Pen, and excuse thy silence. What is it that hath so sorely bewildered thee?

The inebriation of Thy presence, O Well-Beloved of all worlds, hath seized and possessed me.

Arise, and proclaim unto the entire creation the tidings that He Who is the All-Merciful hath directed His steps towards the Riḍván and entered it. Guide, then, the people unto the garden of delight which God hath made the Throne of His Paradise. We have chosen thee to be our most mighty Trumpet, whose blast is to signalize the resurrection of all mankind.

Say: This is the Paradise on whose foliage the wine of utterance hath imprinted the testimony: "He that was hidden from the eyes of men is revealed, girded with sovereignty and power!" This is the Paradise, the rustling of whose leaves proclaims: "O ye that inhabit the heavens and the earth! There hath appeared what hath never previously appeared. He Who, from everlasting, had concealed His Face from the sight of creation is now come." From the whispering breeze that wafteth amidst its branches there cometh the cry: "He Who is the sovereign Lord of all is made manifest. The Kingdom is God's," while from its streaming waters can be heard the murmur: "All eyes are gladdened, for He Whom none hath beheld, Whose secret no one hath discovered, hath lifted the veil of glory, and uncovered the countenance of Beauty."

Within this Paradise, and from the heights of its loftiest chambers, the Maids of Heaven have cried out and shouted: "Rejoice, ye dwellers of the realms above, for the fingers of Him Who is the Ancient of Days are ringing, in the name of the All-Glorious, the Most Great Bell, in the midmost heart of the heavens. The hands of bounty have borne round the cup of everlasting life. Approach, and quaff your fill. Drink with healthy relish, O ye that are the very incarnations of longing, ye who are the embodiments of vehement desire!"

This is the Day whereon He Who is the Revealer of the names of God hath stepped out of the Tabernacle of glory, and proclaimed unto all who are in the heavens and all who are on earth: "Put away the cups of Paradise and all the life-giving waters they contain, for lo, the people of Bahá have entered the blissful abode of the Divine Presence, and quaffed the wine of reunion, from the chalice of the beauty of their Lord, the All-Possessing, the Most High."

Forget the world of creation, O Pen, and turn thou towards the face of thy Lord, the Lord of all names. Adorn, then, the world with the ornament of the favors of thy Lord, the King of everlasting days. For We perceive the fragrance of the Day whereon He Who is the Desire of all nations hath shed upon the kingdoms of the unseen and of the seen the splendor of the light of His most excellent names, and enveloped them with the radiance of the luminaries of His most gracious favors—favors which none can reckon except Him, Who is the omnipotent Protector of the entire creation.

Look not upon the creatures of God except with the eye of kindliness and of mercy, for Our loving providence hath pervaded all created things, and Our grace encompassed the earth and the heavens. This is the Day whereon the true servants of God partake of the life-giving waters of reunion, the Day whereon those that are nigh unto Him are able to drink of the soft-flowing river of immortality, and they who believe in His unity, the wine of His Presence, through their recognition of Him Who is the Highest and Last End of all, in Whom the Tongue of Majesty and Glory voiceth the call: "The Kingdom is Mine. I, Myself, am, of Mine own right, its Ruler."

Attract the hearts of men, through the call of Him, the one alone Beloved. Say: This is the Voice of

God, if ye do but hearken. This is the Day Spring of the Revelation of God, did ye but know it. This is the Dawning-Place of the Cause of God, were ye to recognize it. This is the Source of the commandment of God, did ye but judge it fairly. This is the manifest and hidden Secret; would that ye might perceive it. O peoples of the world! Cast away, in My name that transcendeth all other names, the things ye possess, and immerse yourselves in this Ocean in whose depths lay hidden the pearls of wisdom and of utterance, an ocean that surgeth in My name, the All-Merciful. Thus instructeth you He with Whom is the Mother Book.

The Best-Beloved is come. In His right hand is the sealed Wine of His name. Happy is the man that turneth unto Him, and drinketh his fill, and exclaimeth: "Praise be to Thee, O Revealer of the signs of God!" By the righteousness of the Almighty! Every hidden thing hath been manifested through the power of truth. All the favors of God have been sent down, as a token of His grace. The waters of everlasting life have, in their fullness, been proffered unto men. Every single cup hath been borne round by the hand of the Well-Beloved. Draw near, and tarry not, though it be for one short moment.

Blessed are they that have soared on the wings of detachment and attained the station which, as ordained by God, overshadoweth the entire creation, whom neither the vain imaginations of the learned, nor the multitude of the hosts of the earth have succeeded in deflecting from His Cause. Who is there among you, O people, who will renounce the world, and draw nigh unto God, the Lord of all names? Where is he to be found who, through the power of My name that transcendeth all created things, will cast away the things that men possess, and cling, with all his might, to the things which God, the Knower of the unseen and of the seen, hath bidden him observe? Thus hath His bounty been sent down unto men, His testimony fulfilled, and His proof shone forth above the Horizon of mercy. Rich is the prize that shall be won by him who hath believed and exclaimed: "Lauded art Thou, O Beloved of all worlds! Magnified be Thy name, O Thou the Desire of every understanding heart!"

Rejoice with exceeding gladness, O people of Bahá, as ye call to remembrance the Day of supreme felicity, the Day whereon the Tongue of the Ancient of Days hath spoken, as He departed from His House, proceeding to the Spot from which He shed upon the whole of creation the splendors of His name, the All-Merciful. God is Our witness. Were We to reveal the hidden secrets of that Day, all they that dwell on earth and in the heavens would swoon away and die, except such as will be preserved by God, the Almighty, the All-Knowing, the All-Wise.

Such is the inebriating effect of the words of God upon Him Who is the Revealer of His undoubted proofs, that His Pen can move no longer. With these words He concludeth His Tablet: "No God is there but Me, the Most Exalted, the Most Powerful, the Most Excellent, the All-Knowing."

Release yourselves, O nightingales of God, from the thorns and brambles of wretchedness and misery, and wing your flight to the rose-garden of unfading splendor. O My friends that dwell upon the dust! Haste forth unto your celestial habitation. Announce unto yourselves the joyful tidings: "He Who is the Best-Beloved is come! He hath crowned Himself with the glory of God's Revelation, and hath unlocked to the face of men the doors of His ancient Paradise." Let all eyes rejoice, and let every ear be gladdened, for now is the time to gaze on His beauty, now is the fit time to hearken to His voice. Proclaim unto every longing lover: "Behold, your Well-Beloved hath come among men!" and to the messengers of the Monarch of love impart the tidings: "Lo, the Adored One hath appeared arrayed in the fullness of His glory!" O lovers of His beauty! Turn the anguish of your separation from Him into the joy of an everlasting reunion, and let the sweetness of His presence dissolve the bitterness of your remoteness from His court.

Behold how the manifold grace of God which is being showered from the clouds of Divine glory, hath, in this day, encompassed the world. For whereas in days past every lover besought and searched after his Beloved, it is the Beloved Himself Who now is calling His lovers and is inviting them to attain His presence. Take heed lest ye forfeit so precious a favor; beware lest ye belittle so remarkable a token of His grace. Abandon not the incorruptible benefits, and be not content with that which perisheth. Lift up the veil that obscureth your vision, and dispel the darkness with which it is enveloped, that ye may gaze on the naked beauty of the Beloved's face, may behold that which no eye hath beheld, and hear that which no ear hath heard.

Hear Me, ye mortal birds! In the Rose Garden of changeless splendor a Flower hath begun to bloom, compared to which every other flower is but a thorn, and before the brightness of Whose glory the very essence of beauty must pale and wither. Arise, therefore, and, with the whole enthusiasm of your hearts, with all the eagerness of your souls, the full fervor of your will, and the concentrated efforts of your entire being, strive to attain the paradise of His presence, and endeavor to inhale the fragrance of the incorruptible Flower, to breathe the sweet savors of holiness, and to obtain a portion of this perfume of celestial glory. Whoso followeth this counsel will break his chains asunder, will taste the abandonment of enraptured love, will attain unto his heart's desire, and will surrender his soul into the hands of his Beloved. Bursting through his cage, he will, even as the bird of the spirit, wing his flight to his holy and everlasting nest.

Night hath succeeded day, and day hath succeeded night, and the hours and moments of your lives have come and gone, and yet none of you hath, for one instant, consented to detach himself from that which perisheth. Bestir yourselves, that the brief moments that are still yours may not be dissipated and lost. Even as the swiftness of lightning your days shall pass, and your bodies shall be laid to rest beneath a canopy of dust. What can ye then achieve? How can ye atone for your past failure?

The everlasting Candle shineth in its naked glory. Behold how it hath consumed every mortal veil. O ye moth-like lovers of His light! Brave every danger, and consecrate your souls to its consuming flame. O ye that thirst after Him! Strip yourselves of every earthly affection, and hasten to embrace your Beloved. With a zest that none can equal make haste to attain unto Him. The Flower, thus far hidden from the sight of men, is unveiled to your eyes. In the open radiance of His glory He standeth before you. His voice summoneth all the holy and sanctified beings to come and be united with Him. Happy is he that turneth thereunto; well is it with him that hath attained, and gazed on the light of so wondrous a countenance.

On the First Day of Riḍván, Bahá'u'lláh revealed the Surih of Patience (Súriy-i ṣabr), *also known as the Tablet of Job* (Lawḥ-i ayyúb). *Shoghi Effendi has translated a brief passage from that work:*

In the Súriy-i-Ṣabr, revealed as far back as the year 1863, on the very first day of [Bahá'u'lláh's] arrival in the garden of Riḍván, He thus affirms: *"God hath sent down His Messengers to succeed to Moses and Jesus, and He will continue to do so till 'the end that hath no end'; so that His grace may, from the heaven of Divine bounty, be continually vouchsafed to mankind."*

Days of Riḍván

words of 'Abdu'l-Bahá

The following remarks are selected from a talk given by 'Abdu'l-Bahá on April 18, 1912 in New York, at the home of Mr. and Mrs. Marshall L. Emery:

In truth, the Blessed Perfection was a refuge for every weak one, a shelter for every fearing one, kind to every indigent one, lenient and loving to all creatures.

He became well-known in regard to these qualities before the Báb appeared. Then Bahá'u'lláh declared the Báb's mission to be true and promulgated His teachings. The Báb announced that the greater Manifestation would take place after Him and called the Promised One "Him Whom God shall make manifest," saying that nine years later the reality of His own mission would become apparent. In His writings He stated that in the ninth year this expected One would be known; in the ninth year they would attain to all glory and felicity; in the ninth year they would advance rapidly. Between Bahá'u'lláh and the Báb there was communication privately. The Báb wrote a letter containing three hundred and sixty derivatives of the root *Bahá*.

The Báb was martyred in Tabriz; and Bahá'u'lláh, exiled into Iraq in 1852, announced Himself in Baghdad. For the Persian government had decided that as long as He remained in Persia the peace of the country would be disturbed; therefore, He was exiled in the expectation that Persia would become quiet. His banishment, however, produced the opposite effect. New tumult arose, and the mention of His greatness and influence spread everywhere throughout the country. The proclamation of His manifestation and mission was made in Baghdad. He called His friends together there and spoke to them of God.

'Abdu'l-Bahá delivered this talk to the Bahá'ís in Washington, D.C., on the First Day of Riḍván, April 21, 1912:

In this present cycle there will be an evolution in civilization unparalleled in the history of the world. The world of humanity has, heretofore, been in the stage of infancy; now it is approaching maturity. Just as the individual human organism, having attained the period of maturity, reaches its fullest degree of physical strength and ripened intellectual faculties so that in one year of this ripened period there is witnessed an unprecedented measure of development, likewise the world of humanity in this cycle of its completeness and consummation will realize an immeasurable upward progress, and that power of accomplishment whereof each individual human reality is the depository of God—that outworking Universal Spirit—like the intellectual faculty, will reveal itself in infinite degrees of perfection.

Therefore, thank ye God that ye have come into

the plane of existence in this radiant century wherein the bestowals of God are appearing from all directions, when the doors of the Kingdom have been opened unto you, the call of God is being raised, and the virtues of the human world are in the process of unfoldment. The day has come when all darkness is to be dispelled, and the Sun of Truth shall shine forth radiantly. This time of the world may be likened to the equinoctial in the annual cycle. For, verily, this is the spring season of God. In the Holy Books a promise is given that the springtime of God shall make itself manifest; Jerusalem, the Holy City, shall descend from heaven; Zion shall leap forth and dance; and the Holy Land shall be submerged in the ocean of divine effulgence.

At the time of the vernal equinox in the material world a wonderful vibrant energy and new life-quickening is observed everywhere in the vegetable kingdom; the animal and human kingdoms are resuscitated and move forward with a new impulse. The whole world is born anew, resurrected. Gentle zephyrs are set in motion, wafting and fragrant; flowers bloom; the trees are in blossom, the air temperate and delightful; how pleasant and beautiful become the mountains, fields and meadows. Likewise, the spiritual bounty and springtime of God quicken the world of humanity with a new animus and vivification. All the virtues which have been deposited and potential in human hearts are being revealed from that Reality as flowers and blossoms from divine gardens. It is a day of joy, a time of happiness, a period of spiritual growth. I beg of God that this divine spiritual civilization may have the fullest impression and effect upon you. May you become as growing plants. May the trees of your hearts bring forth new leaves and variegated blossoms. May ideal fruits appear from them in order that the world of humanity, which has grown and developed in material civilization, may be quickened in the bringing forth of spiritual ideals. Just as human intellects have revealed the secrets of matter and have brought forth from the realm of the invisible the mysteries of nature, may minds and spirits, likewise, come into the knowledge of the verities of God, and the realities of the Kingdom be made manifest in human hearts. Then the world will be the paradise of Abhá, the standard of the Most Great Peace will be borne aloft, and the oneness of the world of humanity in all its beauty, glory and significance will become apparent.

The following passage is taken from a Tablet of 'Abdu'l-Bahá written to a Bahá'í woman in Britain:

Thou didst wish to celebrate the Day of Riḍván with a feast, and to have those present on that day engage in reciting Tablets with delight and joy, and thou didst request me to send thee a letter to be read on that day. My letter is this:

O ye beloved, and ye handmaids of the Merciful! This is the day when the Day-Star of Truth rose over the horizon of life, and its glory spread, and its brightness shone out with such power that it clove the dense and high-piled clouds and mounted the skies of the world in all its splendor. Hence do ye witness a new stirring throughout all created things.

See how, in this day, the scope of sciences and arts hath widened out, and what wondrous technical advances have been made, and to what a high degree the mind's powers have increased, and what stupendous inventions have appeared.

This age is indeed as a hundred other ages: should

ye gather the yield of a hundred ages, and set that against the accumulated product of our times, the yield of this one era will prove greater than that of a hundred gone before. Take ye, for example, the sum total of all the books that were ever written in ages past, and compare that with the books and treatises, that our era hath produced: these books, written in our day alone, far and away exceeded the total number of volumes that have been written down the ages. See how powerful is the influence exerted by the Day-Star of the world upon the inner essence of all created things!

But alas, a thousand times alas! The eyes see it not, the ears are deaf, and the hearts and minds are oblivious of this supreme bestowal. Strive ye then, with all your hearts and souls, to awaken those who slumber, to cause the blind to see, and the dead to rise.

The Declaration of
Bahá'u'lláh's Mission
by Shoghi Effendi

A BAGHDAD SQUARE
in the nineteenth century.

The effect upon the colony of exiles of this sudden intelligence [of the order for Bahá'u'lláh's banishment to Constantinople] was instantaneous and overwhelming. "That day," wrote an eyewitness, describing the reaction of the community to the news of Bahá'u'lláh's approaching departure, "witnessed a commotion associated with the turmoil of the Day of Resurrection. Methinks, the very gates and walls of the city wept aloud at their imminent separation from the Abhá Beloved. The first night mention was made of His intended departure His loved ones, one and all, renounced both sleep and food. . . . Not a soul amongst them could be tranquillized. Many had resolved that in the event of their being deprived of the bounty of accompanying Him, they would, without hesitation, kill themselves. . . . Gradually, however, through the words which He addressed them, and through His exhortations and His loving-kindness, they were calmed and resigned themselves to His good-pleasure." For every one of them, whether Arab or Persian, man or woman, child or adult, who lived in Ba<u>gh</u>dád, He revealed during those days, in His own hand, a separate Tablet. In most of these Tablets He predicted the appearance of the *"Calf"* and of the *"Birds of the Night,"* allusions to those who, as anticipated in the Tablet of the Holy Mariner, . . . were to raise the standard of rebellion and precipitate the gravest crisis in the history of the Faith.

Twenty-seven days after that mournful Tablet [of the Holy Mariner] had been so unexpectedly revealed by Bahá'u'lláh, and the fateful communication, presaging His departure to Constantinople had been delivered into His hands on a Wednesday afternoon (April 22, 1863), thirty-one days after Naw-Rúz, on the third of <u>Dh</u>i'l-Qa'dih, 1279 A.H., He set forth on the first stage of His four months' journey to the capital of the Ottoman Empire. That historic day, forever after designated as the first day of the Riḍván Festival, the culmination of innumerable farewell visits which friends and acquaintances of every class and denomination, had been paying Him, was one the like of which the inhabitants of Ba<u>gh</u>dád had rarely beheld. A concourse of people of both sexes and of every age, comprising friends and strangers, Arabs, Kurds, and Persians, notables and clerics, officials and merchants, as well as many of the lower classes, the poor, the orphaned, the outcast, some surprised, others heartbroken, many tearful and apprehensive,

THE DECLARATION OF BAHÁ'U'LLÁH'S MISSION

a few impelled by curiosity or secret satisfaction, thronged the approaches of His house, eager to catch a final glimpse of One Who, for a decade, had, through precept and example, exercised so potent an influence on so large a number of the heterogeneous inhabitants of their city.

Leaving for the last time, amidst weeping and lamentation, His *"Most Holy Habitation,"* out of which had *"gone forth the breath of the All-Glorious,"* and from which had poured forth, in *"ceaseless strains,"* the *"melody of the All-Merciful,"* and dispensing on His way with a lavish hand a last alms to the poor He had so faithfully befriended, and uttering words of comfort to the disconsolate who besought Him on every side, He, at length, reached the banks of the river, and was ferried across, accompanied by His sons and amanuensis, to the Najíbíyyih Garden, situated on the opposite shore. *"O My companions,"* He thus addressed the faithful band that surrounded Him before He embarked, *"I entrust to your keeping this city of Ba<u>gh</u>dád, in the state ye now behold it, when from the eyes of friends and strangers alike, crowding its housetops, its streets and markets, tears like the rain of spring are flowing down, and I depart. With you it now rests to watch lest your deeds and conduct dim the flame of love that gloweth within the breasts of its inhabitants."*

The muezzin had just raised the afternoon call to

prayer when Bahá'u'lláh entered the Najíbíyyih Garden, where He tarried twelve days before His final departure from the city. There His friends and companions, arriving in successive waves, attained His presence and bade Him, with feelings of profound sorrow, their last farewell.

The arrival of Bahá'u'lláh in the Najíbíyyih Garden, subsequently designated by His followers the Garden of Riḍván, signalizes the commencement of what has come to be recognized as the holiest and most significant of all Bahá'í festivals, the festival commemorating the Declaration of His Mission to His companions. So momentous a Declaration may well be regarded both as the logical consummation of that revolutionizing process which was initiated by Himself upon His return from Sulaymáníyyih, and as a prelude to the final proclamation of that same Mission to the world and its rulers from Adrianople.

Through that solemn act the *"delay,"* of no less than a decade, divinely interposed between the birth of Bahá'u'lláh's Revelation in the Síyáh-Chál and its announcement to the Báb's disciples, was at long last terminated. The *"set time of concealment,"* during which as He Himself has borne witness, the *"signs and tokens of a divinely-appointed Revelation"* were being showered upon Him, was fulfilled. The *"myriad veils of light,"* within which His glory had been

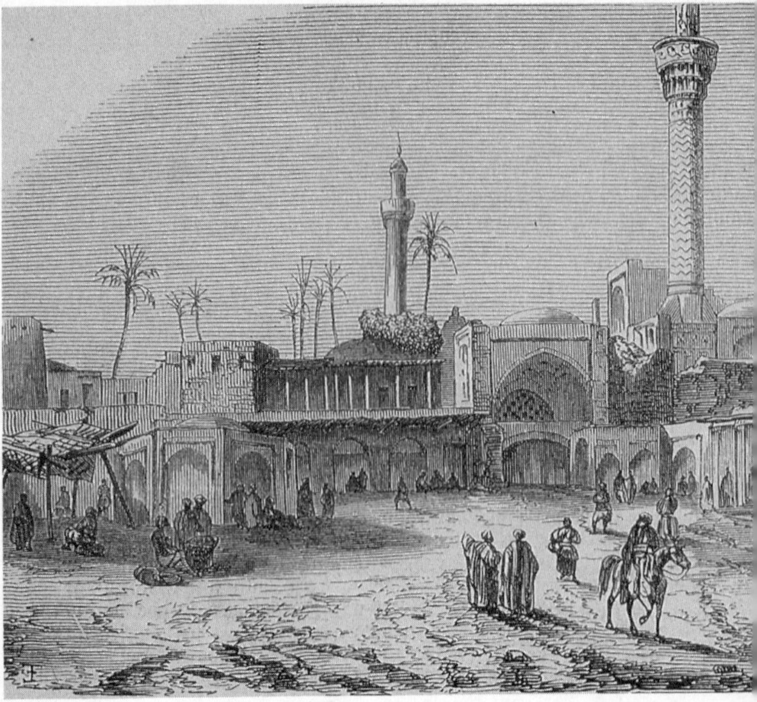

A BAGHDAD STREET
circa 1857.

wrapped, were, at that historic hour, partially lifted, vouchsafing to mankind *"an infinitesimal glimmer"* of the effulgence of His *"peerless, His most sacred and exalted Countenance."* The *"thousand two hundred and ninety days,"* fixed by Daniel in the last chapter of His Book, as the duration of the *"abomination that maketh desolate"* had now elapsed. The *"hundred lunar years,"* destined to immediately precede that blissful consummation (1335 days), announced by Daniel in that same chapter, had commenced. The nineteen years, constituting the first "Váhid," pre-ordained in the Persian Bayán by the pen of the Báb, had been completed. The Lord of the Kingdom, Jesus Christ returned in the glory of the Father, was about to ascend His throne, and assume the scepter of a world-embracing, indestructible sovereignty. The community of the Most Great Name, the *"companions of the Crimson Colored Ark,"* lauded in glowing terms in the Qayyúmu'l-Asmá', had visibly emerged. The Báb's own prophecy regarding the *"Riḍván,"* the scene of the unveiling of Bahá'u'lláh's transcendent glory, had been literally fulfilled.

Undaunted by the prospect of the appalling adversities which, as predicted by Himself, were soon to overtake Him; on the eve of a second banishment which would be fraught with many hazards and perils, and would bring Him still farther from His native land, the cradle of His Faith, to a country alien

THE DECLARATION OF BAHÁ'U'LLÁH'S MISSION

in race, in language and in culture; acutely conscious of the extension of the circle of His adversaries, among whom were soon to be numbered a monarch more despotic than Náṣiri'd-Dín Sháh, and ministers no less unyielding in their hostility than either Ḥájí Mírzá Áqásí or the Amír-Niẓám; undeterred by the perpetual interruptions occasioned by the influx of a host of visitors who thronged His tent, Bahá'u'lláh chose in that critical and seemingly unpropitious hour to advance so challenging a claim, to lay bare the mystery surrounding His person, and to assume, in their plenitude, the power and the authority which were the exclusive privileges of the One Whose advent the Báb had prophesied.

Already the shadow of that great oncoming event had fallen upon the colony of exiles, who awaited expectantly its consummation. As the year *"eighty"* steadily and inexorably approached, He Who had become the real leader of that community increasingly experienced, and progressively communicated to His future followers, the onrushing influences of its informing force. The festive, the soul-entrancing odes which He revealed almost every day; the Tablets, replete with hints, which streamed from His pen; the allusions which, in private converse and public discourse, He made to the approaching hour; the exaltation which in moments of joy and sadness alike flooded His soul; the ecstasy which filled His lovers,

THE DECLARATION OF BAHÁ'U'LLÁH'S MISSION

already enraptured by the multiplying evidences of His rising greatness and glory; the perceptible change noted in His demeanor; and finally, His adoption of the táj (tall felt head-dress), on the day of His departure from His Most Holy House—all proclaimed unmistakably His imminent assumption of the prophetic office and of His open leadership of the community of the Báb's followers.

"Many a night," writes Nabíl, depicting the tumult that had seized the hearts of Bahá'u'lláh's compansions, in the days prior to the declaration of His mission, "would Mírzá Áqá Ján gather them together in his room, close the door, light numerous camphorated candles, and chant aloud to them the newly revealed odes and Tablets in his possession. Wholly oblivious of this contingent world, completely immersed in the realms of the spirit, forgetful of the necessity for food, sleep or drink, they would suddenly discover that night had become day, and that the sun was approaching its zenith."

Of the exact circumstances attending that epoch-making Declaration we, alas, are but scantily informed. The words Bahá'u'lláh actually uttered on that occasion, the manner of His Declaration, the reaction it produced, its impact on Mírzá Yaḥyá, the identity of those who were privileged to hear Him, are shrouded in an obscurity which future historians will find it difficult to penetrate. The frag-

THE DECLARATION OF BAHÁ'U'LLÁH'S MISSION

mentary description left to posterity by His chronicler Nabíl is one of the very few authentic records we possess of the memorable days He spent in that garden. "Every day," Nabíl has related, "ere the hour of dawn, the gardeners would pick the roses which lined the four avenues of the garden, and would pile them in the center of the floor of His blessed tent. So great would be the heap that when His companions gathered to drink their morning tea in His presence, they would be unable to see each other across it. All these roses Bahá'u'lláh would, with His own hands, entrust to those whom He dismissed from His presence every morning to be delivered, on His behalf, to His Arab and Persian friends in the city." "One night," he continues, "the ninth night of the waxing moon, I happened to be one of those who watched beside His blessed tent. As the hour of midnight approached, I saw Him issue from His tent, pass by the places where some of His companions were sleeping, and begin to pace up and down the moonlit, flower-bordered avenues of the garden. So loud was the singing of the nightingales on every side that only those who were near Him could hear distinctly His voice. He continued to walk until, pausing in the midst of one of these avenues, He observed: 'Consider these nightingales. So great is their love for these roses, that sleepless from dusk till dawn, they warble their melodies and commune with burning passion with the object of their adoration. How then can those who claim to be afire with the rose-like beauty of the Beloved choose to sleep?' For three successive nights I watched and circled round His blessed tent. Every time I passed by the couch whereon He lay, I would find Him wakeful, and every day, from morn till eventide, I would see Him ceaselessly engaged in conversing with the stream of visitors who kept flowing in from Baghdád. Not once could I discover in the words He spoke any trace of dissimulation."

The departure of Bahá'u'lláh from the Garden of Riḍván, at noon, on the 14th of Dhi'l-Qa'dih 1279 A.H. (May 3, 1863), witnessed scenes of tumultuous enthusiasm no less spectacular, and even more touching, than those which greeted Him when leaving His Most Great House in Baghdád. "The great tumult," wrote an eyewitness, "associated in our minds with the Day of Gathering, the Day of Judgment, we beheld on that occasion. Believers and unbelievers alike sobbed and lamented. The chiefs and notables who had congregated were struck with wonder. Emotions were stirred to such depths as no tongue can describe, nor could any observer escape their contagion."

Mounted on His steed, a red roan stallion of the finest breed, the best His lovers could purchase for Him, and leaving behind Him a bowing multitude of fervent admirers, He rode forth on the first stage of a journey that was to carry Him to the city of Constantinople. "Numerous were the heads," Nabíl himself a witness of that memorable scene, recounts, "which,

BAGHDAD
showing the Tigris River, circa 1857.

Historical Pictures Service

on every side, bowed to the dust at the feet of His horse, and kissed its hoofs, and countless were those who pressed forward to embrace His stirrups." "How great the number of those embodiments of fidelity," testifies a fellow-traveler, "who, casting themselves before that charger, preferred death to separation from their Beloved! Methinks, that blessed steed trod upon the bodies of those pure-hearted souls."

"He (God) *it was,"* Bahá'u'lláh Himself declares, *"Who enabled Me to depart out of the city* (Baghdád), *clothed with such majesty as none, except the denier and the malicious, can fail to acknowledge."* These marks of homage and devotion continued to surround Him until He was installed in Constantinople.

The Account of
the Greatest Holy Leaf

A VIEW OF BAGHDAD
circa 1860.

Historical Pictures Service

In December 1902, Myron Phelps, an American Lawyer, journeyed to 'Akká to investigate the Bahá'í teachings. There he met 'Abdu'l-Bahá and was able, through intermediaries, to interview the Greatest Holy Leaf, 'Abdu'l-Bahá's sister. The following is her account of Bahá'u'lláh's declaration in Baghdad:

"The Governor of Baghdad at this time was a relative of my father,* but his enemy on account of differences in religious opinion and family misunderstandings.† This man, rendered uncomfortable by the sight of my father's increasing fame and influence, exerted himself to effect his removal from Baghdad. He caused representations to be made to the Shah of Persia that, whereas Bahá'u'lláh had been driven out of Persia because of the harm threatened by his presence to the Muhammadan religion in

---

*Bahá'u'lláh.—ED.
†This information may not be accurate. See *The Master in 'Akká*, p. 149, n. 7; *God Passes By*, pp. 131, 142, 149–50; *Bahá'u'lláh: The King of Glory*, pp. 480, 482–83.—ED.

THE ACCOUNT OF THE GREATEST HOLY LEAF

that country, now he was injuring the religion even more in Baghdad, and still exerting his evil influence in Persia; and that therefore he ought to be removed to a place at a greater distance from that country, and one where he could do less harm.

"These representations and suggestions he sent repeatedly to the Court of Persia, until at length the shah was moved to use his influence with the Sultan of Turkey to have the Bábís transferred from Baghdad to Constantinople. An order to this effect was at length made by the sultan.

"When this news came to us, from which we inferred that my father would again be made a prisoner, we were thrown into consternation, fearing another separation. He was summoned before the magistrates. My brother imperiously declared that he would go in his stead; but this our father overruled, and went himself. Great numbers of his followers had assembled about our house, and these witnessed his departure with many demonstrations of grief, feeling that it was possible that he might not return.

"The magistrates expressed great sorrow to my father; they said that they respected and loved him, that they had not instigated the order, but that they were powerless to suspend or modify it, and must proceed with its execution. My father remained in conference with them nearly all day, but could do nothing to avert the catastrophe. When he re-

THE ACCOUNT OF THE GREATEST HOLY LEAF

turned, he told us that we must prepare to set out for Constantinople in two weeks.

"This report was like a death-knell to his followers, who were still gathered about the house. Many of them were Arabs; their fierce natures rebelled and they gave way to violent remonstrances. They implored the Blessed Perfection* not to desert them. 'You are our shepherd,' they said; 'without you we must die.'

"The next day they so overran the house that we could not prepare for the journey. Then the Blessed Perfection proposed to go with 'Abbás Effendi† to the garden of one of our friends‡ and live there in a tent till the time of departure, that the family might be able to proceed with the packing. This remark was repeated and misunderstood, and the rumor circulated among the believers that the Blessed Perfection was to be taken away alone. Then they came pouring in by hundreds, so wild with grief that they could not be pacified; and when my father started to leave the house with my brother they threw themselves upon the ground before him. One man who had an only child, which had come to him late in his life,

---

*One of the titles of Bahá'u'lláh.—ED.
†'Abdu'l-Bahá.—ED.
‡The Najíbiyyih Garden, now known to Bahá'ís as the Garden of Riḍván.—ED.

stripped the clothes from the child's body and placing it at my father's feet cried, 'Naked I give you my child, my precious child, to do with as you will; only promise not to leave us in distress. Without you we cannot live.'

"Then, as the only way in which to soothe his followers, the Blessed Perfection took all his family to the garden, leaving to friends the preparation of his household goods for the journey. Here we pitched tents and lived in them for two weeks.* The tents made, as it were, a little village, that of my father, which, he occupied alone, in the center.

"Four days before the caravan was to set out, the Blessed Perfection called 'Abbás Effendi into his tent and told him that he himself was the one whose coming had been promised by the Báb—the Chosen of God, the Center of the Covenant. A little later, and before leaving the garden, he selected from among his disciples four others, to whom he made the same declaration. He further said to these five that for the present he enjoined upon them secrecy as to this communication, as the time had not come for a public declaration; but that there were reasons which caused him to deem it necessary to make it at that time to a few whom he could trust. . . .

---

*Actually, twelve days: the Festival of Riḍván, April 21 to May 2, commemorates this period.—ED.

THE ACCOUNT OF THE GREATEST HOLY LEAF

"Many of the Blessed Perfection's followers decided to abandon Baghdad also, and accompany him in his wanderings. When the caravan started, our company numbered about seventy-five persons. All the young men, and others who could ride, were mounted on horses. The women and the Blessed Perfection were furnished wagons. We were accompanied by a military escort. This journey took place in 1863, about eleven years after our arrival in Baghdad."

The Spoken Chronicle of
Mírzá Asadu'lláh Ká<u>sh</u>ání

A VIEW OF BAGHDAD on the Tigris River, circa 1860.

Historical Pictures Service

Mírzá Asadu'lláh Ká<u>sh</u>ání, one of the Bahá'ís who joined Bahá'u'lláh in exile in Baghdad and remained in the city after He departed, has left this account of his experiences in the Garden of Riḍván:

Whilst Bahá'u'lláh was encamped in the Riḍván, there was much wind for some days.

His tent swayed; we thought it might be blown down, therefore we took it in turns to sit and hold the tent ropes so that it might be steady; night and day we held the ropes, so glad, in this way, to be near our Glorious Lord.

All the city came, friends and others, to see Him leave for the Riḍván. There was a great crowd. Weeping women pressed forward and laid their babes and young children at His feet. He tenderly raised those infants, one by one, blessing them, gently and lovingly replacing them in their sorrowing mothers' arms, and charging them to bring up those dear flowers of humanity to serve God in steadfast faith and truth.

CHRONICLE OF MÍRZÁ ASADU'LLÁH KÁSHÁNÍ

What a soul-stirring day!

Men threw themselves in His path; if only His blessed feet might touch them as He passed.

Our Beloved One got into a boat to cross the river, the people pressing round Him waiting, not to lose one of the remaining chances of being in His Presence.

At length the boat put off, and we watched it with sorrowing hearts.

Then we were aware of an extraordinary exhilaration, some marvelous exaltation in the atmosphere of that day.

The reason for this phenomenon we were in due time to learn.

When we had seen that the boat was on the other side of the river, we started off to walk to the Riḍván, where we set up His tent, and five or six others for the friends. I helped Mírzá Muḥammad Báqir to cook, and to make tea for the friends.

The family of Bahá'u'lláh joined Him in the Riḍván on the ninth day; and on the twelfth day, in the afternoon, they went from us, under the escort of Turkish soldiers to an unknown destination.

Although Bahá'u'lláh had commanded the friends not to follow them, I was so loath to let Him go out of my sight, that I ran after them for three hours.

He saw me, and getting down from His horse, waited for me, telling me with His beautiful voice,

CHRONICLE OF MÍRZÁ ASADU'LLÁH KÁSHÁNÍ

full of love and kindness, to go back to Baghdad, and, with the friends, to set about our work, not slothfully, but with energy:

"Be not overcome with sorrow—I am leaving friends I love in Baghdad. I will surely send to them tidings of our welfare. Be steadfast in your service to God, who doeth whatsoever He willeth. Live in such peace as will be permitted to you."

We watched them disappear into the darkness with sinking hearts, for their enemies were powerful and cruel! And we knew not where they were being taken.

An unknown destination!

Weeping bitterly, we turned our faces toward Baghdad, determining to live according to His command.

We had not been, at that time, informed of the great event of the "Declaration," that our revered and beloved Bahá'u'lláh was He Who should come—"He Whom God shall make Manifest"—but we again felt that unspeakable joy, which surged within us, overcoming our bitter sorrow, with a great and mysterious radiancy.

Before the departure, the Governor of Baghdad had come to offer his services. "Is there not anything I can do?"

Bahá'u'lláh replied:

"One thing I ask of thee—protect the friends after I am gone. This only I wish from thee."

The Memoirs of
Ustád Muḥammad-'Alí Salmání

❧

A STREET IN BAGHDAD
in the nineteenth century.

Historical Pictures Service

Muḥammad-'Alí Salmání was an unlettered believer who chose to share Bahá'u'lláh's exile in Baghdad, where he acted as His barber. He also served as Bahá'u'lláh's attendant in the Persian bathhouse, where this story begins:

Another time, when I was about to make use of the rubbing mitt, Bahá'u'lláh said, "Ustád Muḥammad-'Alí, we have in mind to take a long journey. What do you say to that?"

I bowed. And that day went by.

Two days later, He said He was about to go to Government House. This terrified me. I went and fastened on a dagger, concealed a couple of pistols about me, and left for the seat of government to see what was happening. I went over the bridge and walked past the confectionary shop of Siyyid Ḥusayn of Isfahan—and there I saw Áqáy-i Kalím.* He called to me, and I asked him what was going on. He replied that Bahá'u'lláh had been summoned. Not much

*Bahá'u'lláh's faithful half brother.—ED.

MEMOIRS OF USTÁD MUḤAMMAD-'ALÍ SALMÁNÍ

time passed before the Blessed Beauty returned, and we learned that orders had come from Istanbul to Baghdad, that Bahá'u'lláh should proceed to wherever He might desire, away from Baghdad; the choice was to be His, that is, within the Ottoman territory.

It became widely known that Ḥájí Mírzá Ḥusayn Khán* was behind this proposal. He had said, "Because of the proximity of Baghdad to Persian soil, the Cause of Bahá is constantly progressing."

Námiq Páshá had sent the following message to Bahá'u'lláh: "This decree has already been received here ten or twelve times, but I did not tell you of it, and my reply to it was: 'Bahá'u'lláh has lived in Baghdad twelve years,† and up to now no fault has ever been found in Him.'"

Bahá'u'lláh had said to the messenger: "Tell Námiq Páshá that I will not come to the Government House, but I will come to the mosque in its vicinity. I will meet there with whoever wishes to address me."

Bahá'u'lláh went to the mosque, and the deputy of Námiq Páshá appeared and said, "Námiq had desired to come to You himself, but he was ashamed to, and sent me in his place." He then recited the particulars of the decree.

---

*The Persian ambassador to Istanbul.—ED.
†Actually, ten years. Bahá'u'lláh arrived in Baghdad from Tehran in April 1853, and departed for Istanbul in April 1863. —ED.

The Beloved said, "I will go to Istanbul." And they approved.

Afterward, thinking of the journey, Bahá'u'lláh said, "I will go alone." But the Household wept and insisted and begged. He finally agreed that they should accompany Him, and He named those who were to stay behind. One night Mírzá Muḥammad-Qulí came in and told me: "He says that you must be among the ones who go with Him."

After some days, Bahá'u'lláh proceeded to a garden outside the city, and there His tent was pitched. This was the garden of Najíb Páshá [later known as the Garden of Riḍván] and it was here in this garden that He openly declared His Mission. That is, He spoke of the manifestation of the Exalted One, the Báb, saying that He was the Qá'im,* that the Cause was His Cause—and at the same time, with certain intimations, He also declared His own Mission. During the twelve days of His sojourn in that garden, every morning and every afternoon He would speak of the Báb's Cause and declare His own.

---

*The Promised One.—ED.

Appendix

Bahá'í Holy Days

The Bahá'í day starts and ends at sunset, and consequently the date of the celebration of Bahá'í feasts should be adjusted to conform to the Bahá'í calendar time. For further particulars on this subject you should refer to the section entitled "Bahá'í Calendar" in *The Bahá'í World*.

The Guardian would advise that, if feasible, the Friends should commemorate certain of the feasts and anniversaries at the following time:

The anniversary of the Declaration of the Báb on 22 May, at about two hours after sunset.

The first day of Riḍván, at about 3 p.m. on 21 April.

The anniversary of the Martyrdom of the Báb on 9 July, at about noon.

The anniversary of the Ascension of Bahá'u'lláh on 29 May, at 3 a.m.

The Ascension of 'Abdu'l-Bahá on 28 November, at 1 a.m.

The other anniversaries the believers are free to gather at any time during the day which they find convenient.

(From a letter written on behalf of Shoghi Effendi, quoted in Principles of Bahá'í Administration *[London: Bahá'í Publishing Trust, 1950] p. 56)*

APPENDIX

The first day of Riḍván, according to the Sacred Texts, falls 31 days after Naw-Rúz, on the 13th day of the month of Jalál. It so happened that in 1863 Naw-Rúz coincided with 22nd March, therefore Riḍván was from 22nd April to 3rd May. As Shoghi Effendi has explained in a letter to your Assembly dated 15 May 1940 ("Bahá'í News" No. 138, p. 1), the fixing of the date of Naw-Rúz for each year is dependent upon the Universal House of Justice's determining which spot on earth is to be regarded as the standard. Pending such a decision the Persian Bahá'ís have always celebrated Naw-Rúz in accordance with the date of the spring equinox in that country, while the western friends have observed the beginning of the Bahá'í year in accordance with the Gregorian Calendar so that Naw-Rúz has usually fallen on 21st March. Similarly, the western friends have observed the other Bahá'í Holy Days in accordance with their Gregorian anniversaries, while the eastern believers have observed some in accordance with the solar calendar and others in accordance with the lunar calendar. All these matters will be dealt with by the Universal House of Justice in due course.

(From a letter of the Universal House of Justice to the National Spiritual Assembly of the Bahá'ís of the United States, November 11, 1989)

Sources

Tablets Revealed for Riḍván, from Shoghi Effendi, *God Passes By* (Wilmette, Ill.: Bahá'í Publishing Trust, 1944) pp. 153–54; *Gleanings from the Writings of Bahá'u'lláh* (Wilmette, Ill.: Bahá'í Publishing Trust, 1939) pp. 27–35; ibid., pp. 319–22; *World Order of Bahá'u'lláh* (Wilmette, Ill., Bahá'í Publishing Trust, 1938 [1974]), p. 116.

Days of Riḍván, from *The Promulgation of Universal Peace: Talks Delivered by 'Abdu'l-Bahá during His Visit to the United States and Canada in 1912* (Wilmette, Ill.: Bahá'í Publishing Trust, 1922–25 [1982]) p. 26; ibid., pp. 37–39; *Selections from the Writings of 'Abdu'l-Bahá* (Haifa: Bahá'í World Centre, 1978).

The Declaration of Bahá'u'lláh's Mission, from *God Passes By*, pp. 148–49; pp. 151–53; p. 155.

The Account of the Greatest Holy Leaf, from Myron H. Phelps, *Life and Teachings of Abbas Effendi* (New York: G.P. Putnam's Sons, 1903 [reprinted as *The Master in 'Akká* (Los Angeles: Kalimát Press, 1985) pp. 35–39]).

SOURCES

The Spoken Chronicle of Mírzá Asadu'lláh Kashání, from *The Chosen Highway*, comp. by Lady Blomfield (London: Bahá'í Publishing Trust, 1940 [reprinted (Wilmette, Ill. Bahá'í Publishing Trust, 1967)]) pp. 122–23.

The Memoirs of Ustád Muḥammad-'Alí Salmání, from *My Memories of Bahá'u'lláh* (Los Angeles: Kalimát Press, 1982) pp. 20–22.